Also by Dan Gutman

My Weird School
FAST FACTS
Explorers, Presidents, and Toilets

Dan Gutman

Pictures by
Jim Paillot

HARPER
An Imprint of HarperCollinsPublishers

To Emma

Photograph credits: page 5: Library of Congress; 21: Library of Congress; 23: Library of Congress; 53: traveler1116/Getty Images; 56: Liliboas/Getty Images; 57: DKart/Getty Images; 61: L. Cohen/Getty Images; 67: MPI/Getty Images; 70: Hulton Archive/Getty Images; 72: Pgiam/Getty Images; 96: Image Source/Getty Images; 103: Library of Congress; 106: Jupiterimages/Getty Images; 106: ZU_09/Getty Images; 109: Library of Congress; 117: Education Images/UIG; 119: Kim Storup/EyeEm/Getty Images; 131: Library of Congress; 136: Roger Viollet/Getty Images; 138: Bettmann/Getty Images; 143: Courtesy of PDSA; 144: Anthony Potter Collection/Getty Images; 160: Fox Photos/Getty Images; 162: Bettmann/Getty Images; 163: Bettmann/Getty Images; 164: L. Cohen/Getty Images; 177: Choi Won-Suk/Getty Images

The author gratefully acknowledges the editorial contributions of Laurie Calkhoven.

ISBN 978-0-06-230623-4 (trade bdg.)
ISBN 978-0-06-230624-1 (lib. bdg.)

17 18 19 20 21   OPM   10 9 8 7 6 5 4 3 2 1
❖
First Edition

Contents

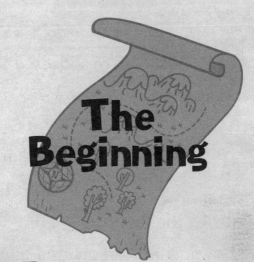

The Beginning

 My name is Andrea and I *love* history!

 Oh no! It's Andrea Young, that annoying girl in my class with curly brown hair! Who said *you* could take over my book?

1

It's *our* book, Arlo!* Not *your* book. We're supposed to talk about history *together.*

 History? Are you kidding me? History is the most boring subject in the history of the world! Nobody wants to read about a bunch of dead guys.

History is fascinating, Arlo! And it's not just about dead guys. When we learn about US history, we're learning about how our country came to be. That's important!

---

* Andrea calls me by my real name because she knows I don't like it. She is annoying.

2

I'll tell you what's important. Tissues! If we didn't have tissues, how would I blow my nose?

 Ignore him. Arlo just wants attention. If he doesn't want to talk about the history of the United States, then I will. He can just sit there and blow his nose if he wants to.

 Nothing doing! I am Professor A.J., and I already forgot more history than Andrea will ever learn. So nah-nah-nah boo-boo on her. I know everything that's worth knowing. For instance, did you know how America came to be discovered? Well, I'll tell you.

It all started in 1492. Columbus told the Pilgrims to go sail to America because he was busy playing video games. The Pilgrims hired George Washington to write the Gettysburg Address in his underwear, and the next thing anybody knew, Neil Armstrong was standing on the moon taking selfies! And that's everything you need to know about American history.

 That's just ridiculous, Arlo, and you know it! *None* of that is true.

 Yeah, but some people will fall for *anything*! That just goes to show that you shouldn't believe everything you read in a book. Especially a My Weird School book! But I know lots of *real* history too. I bet you didn't know that President Calvin Coolidge had

Mrs. Grace Coolidge with Rebecca

a pet raccoon named Rebecca, and he let her roam around the White House. That's a *true* fast fact! Look it up if you don't believe me. I could tell you a lot more cool stuff about American history, but I'd rather blow my nose.

Professor A.J.

(the professor of awesomeness)

The professor of being obnox-ious is more like it. Okay, let's get started. We have a lot of ground to cover. I guess we should start from the beginning.

Chapter 1

Who Discovered America Anyway?

A lot of people think Christopher Columbus discovered North America, but there's a name for those people—dopes! The truth is that Leif Eriksson and the Vikings arrived here almost five centuries *before* Columbus. Five hundred years! That's more years than my grandparents are old. So nah-nah-nah boo-boo on Columbus!

 It's not very nice to call people dopes, but I must admit Arlo is right. Around the year AD 1000, the Vikings sailed all the way from Scandinavia— that's Sweden, Norway, and Denmark—and landed in what we now call Canada.

 They also landed in Minnesota, and started a football team there. It was called the Minnesota Vikings.

 Okay, you made that up, Arlo! The truth is that the Vikings

were not known to be very nice people. Some were pirates who burned villages, killed people, and raided and plundered whatever they wanted.

By the way, the Vikings didn't call themselves Vikings. Nobody knows what they called themselves.

I know what they called themselves: Leif and Eric and Rolf
and Olivia. They called themselves by their
names! The Vikings were weird. Tell me
these fast facts about them aren't weird. . . .

- When Viking leaders died, their bod-
  ies were put in boats with their clothes,
  jewelry, and animals. Then the boats
  were set on fire and pushed out to sea.
  Nice funeral!
- Do you know how Vikings would start
  a fire when they weren't home? They
  would pee on some tree fungus, boil it,
  and mold it into chunks they could take
  with them. The sodium nitrate in the
  pee made it easy to get a fire started.
- Did you ever read *Mr. Burke Is Berserk!*?

Well, the word "berserk" comes from "berserkers," the name given to some terrifying Viking warriors who wore bear or wolf skins and howled in battle like wild animals.

- Erik the Red was Leif Eriksson's father. He murdered somebody and got kicked out of Iceland. Then he sailed west to a big island. It was covered in ice and snow, but Erik wanted other people to come there, so do you know what he named it? Greenland! Ha! What a scam. Some people will fall for anything.

 Those fast facts *are* weird, Arlo. Columbus *did* make four trips from Spain between 1492 and 1503, but he never once set foot in North America. That's true. He explored some Caribbean islands and parts of Central and South America.

 So not only was Columbus five hundred years late, but he also went to the wrong place! That guy had no idea where he was. He thought he'd sailed to Asia. What a dumbhead!

He was lucky though. If Columbus hadn't accidentally bumped into the "New World," his ships would have run out of food and water long before he reached Asia.

I'd also like to mention that Columbus was not a nice man. He was named governor of Hispaniola (which is now Haiti and the Dominican Republic), but when the native islanders didn't give him enough gold, he cut their hands off!

He was *really* not a nice man!

You can say *that* again!

He was *really* not a nice man!

 Arlo, did you know that an eclipse once saved Columbus's life? In 1504, he was stranded in Jamaica, and the natives wouldn't give him food. But Columbus had an almanac, and he knew that there would be a lunar eclipse on February 29. So he convinced the natives that his god would make the moon "rise inflamed with wrath" if they didn't feed him. When the eclipse turned the moon red, the natives rushed to him with food and drink.

Do you know why America is called "America"?

 Because "France" was already taken?

 No! It was named after an Italian explorer named Amerigo Vespucci. He was exploring the coast of South America in 1501, and he described it as a "new world." A German mapmaker read about this, and he made a map of the new land, calling it America. And the rest is US history.

 After Columbus, a bunch of

other explorers came here. Some of them, like Hernán Cortés, were looking for a city made of gold. Cortés never found it.* By the way, if you ever find a city of gold in your backyard, let me know and we can split the loot.

 Not all the explorers were searching for gold. Juan Ponce de León of Spain heard about a fountain of youth that would allow him to live forever. He was searching for it in Florida, but he never found it.

---

* I don't know why he didn't just go to a jewelry store. That would have been a lot easier.

Do you know how we know he didn't find the fountain of youth?

 How?

 Because he died.

 Very funny, Arlo. You know, some of the explorers just wanted to find a way to get to Asia by going through

America. They thought there must be a water route that would connect the Atlantic and Pacific Oceans. They called it the Northwest Passage. Jacques Cartier from France never found it. Henry Hudson from England never found it.

 They should have just taken a plane, a train, or used Google Maps.

 There *were* no trains or planes or Google Maps in those days, dumbhead!

 I knew that.

Native Americans

 Do you want to know who *really* discovered America?

I'm not going to tell you.

Okay, okay, I'll tell you.

It was the Native Americans!

That's right. You may have heard them called "Indians," but the correct term is Native Americans. They have the perfect name because they were *native* to *America*!

So all these fancy explorers from Europe thought they were discovering something new, but the joke was on them, because lots of people were already living here. And they had been living here for thousands of years. In fact, there were *hundreds* of tribes spread out across the Americas, from the Yupik people and Inuit of the North down to the Mayans, Aztecs, and Incas in Mexico and South America.

Inuit family, 1899

 It was that dumbhead Christopher Columbus who started

21

calling them "Indians." He thought he was in the East Indies! What a dope. That guy needed a GPS, bad.

 When the Europeans showed up in America, they brought a lot of stuff the Native Americans had never seen before, like cows, sheep, and pigs. Sadly they also brought diseases like smallpox, which killed millions of Native Americans, who did not have the immunities the Europeans had built over time.

 In the years that followed, relations between Native Americans and descendants of those European settlers were complex and challenging. While some of that remains today, we now recognize the important contributions many Native Americans have made to our country's history. Like Sitting Bull (1831–1890), Geronimo (1829–1909), and Sequoyah. Sequoyah was a Cherokee leader who helped his people develop an alphabet. The Sequoia tree was named after him.

Sitting Bull, 1885

There are lots of Native American words that became part

of the English language: "caribou," "chipmunk," "moccasin," "moose," "muskrat," "opossum," "pecan," "powwow," "raccoon," "skunk," "squaw," "toboggan," and "woodchuck."

And about half of our state names come from Native American words: Alabama, Alaska, Arizona, Connecticut, and Iowa, just to name a few. Illinois means "speak in the regular way." Massachusetts means "about the big hill." Michigan means "large lake." Minnesota means "cloudy water." Missouri means "town of large canoes." Ohio means "good river." Utah means "people of the mountains." Wisconsin means "this stream meanders through something red."

And Delaware means "I need to find a bathroom, fast."

 It does not, Arlo!

 I know, but bathrooms are funny. Hey, do you know any-body who has a Mohawk haircut? They probably don't know that it was named after the Mohawks, one of the tribes of the Iroquois Confederation. By the way, the word "mohawk" means "man-eater."

 Do you know what sport was invented by Native Americans?

It was lacrosse! That's a true fast fact.

 Back in those days, Native Americans didn't have email or texts, you know. The telephone hadn't been invented yet. Do you know how they communicated with each other over long distances? They sent smoke signals! No joke!

Chapter 2

The United States Is Born!

It took a long time, but it finally dawned on those dopey Europeans that America was a cool place, and not just a big landmass that prevented them from getting to India. So they figured they might as well stick around here and establish colonies.

Settlers from Spain formed a colony in Florida. The Dutch settled in New York City (but they called it New Amsterdam). That's where Peter Minuit met with the local Native American chiefs and gave them two boxes of stuff—probably hatchets, cloth, metal posts, and beads—in exchange for the island of Manhattan. No kidding! All that stuff in the boxes was worth about twenty-four dollars.

 Twenty-four bucks for an island! Today, you can't even buy a video game for twenty-four dollars.

 But the country that started

the most of America's thirteen colonies was England. In 1587, settlers from England started a colony on Roanoke Island off the coast of North Carolina. Three years later, some other Englishmen came to visit the colony, and you know what they found?

 What?

 Nothing! The Roanoke colony had completely vanished. Poof! The cabins were gone. The settlers were gone. Their animals were gone. The only thing they found was the word "croatan" carved on a fence post and "cro" carved on a tree. That was weird! The "Lost Colony" was never found. Oooh, creepy!

 In 1607, some other Englishmen founded a settlement on the banks of the James River in Virginia. They called it Jamestown, so it had the perfect name. One settler, John Smith, was captured by the Powhatan tribe. They were going to put him to death when a Powhatan princess named Pocahontas saved his life.

Pocahontas was a nice lady. She learned how to speak English, she gave food to the settlers, and she even married one of them! Isn't that romantic? Maybe *we'll* get married some-day, Arlo.

 Over my dead body!

 In the early 1600s, some other groups from England—the Pilgrims and the Puritans—settled in what is now Massachusetts. Well, the Pilgrims didn't *plan* to go to Massachusetts. They wanted to go to Virginia. But they got blown off course. Oops! They were five hundred miles off!

 That reminds me of the time my family was in the car and

my dad missed the exit on the highway. We had to drive hours out of our way. My mom was so mad she didn't talk to my dad for the rest of the day.

 The local Native Americans helped the Pilgrims stay alive. To give thanks and celebrate the first harvest, they threw a three-day party. It was the first Thanksgiving! You probably think they ate turkey, mashed potatoes, and gravy. Wrong! They probably served deer, goose, duck, stewed pumpkins, and eels.

 Eels? Gross! All that bad food and no football games to watch

on TV? That must have been the worst Thanksgiving in the history of the world.

 People like naming things after themselves. After the British took over New Amsterdam in 1664, they renamed it New York, after the Duke of York. In exchange for a debt, King Charles gave some land to William Penn, and together they named it Pennsylvania.

 Huh, and I thought it was called Pennsylvania because they make pencils there! But it would be cool to have a place named after yourself. If I had some land, I would name it A.J. Town.

Little by little, colonies were established: Massachusetts, New Hampshire, Rhode Island, Connecticut, New York, New Jersey, Pennsylvania, Delaware, Maryland, Virginia, North Carolina, South Carolina, and Georgia. They were the thirteen original colonies.

 After they established all those colonies, you'll never believe in a million hundred years what happened next.

I'm not going to tell you.

Okay, okay, I'll tell you.

But you have to read the next chapter first. So nah-nah-nah boo-boo on you.

The Colonists
Are Revolting!

Do you know how the United States became a separate country from England? Well, here's what happened: One morning, George Washington got out of bed, brushed his fake teeth, and went to his desk. Then he sent an email to his friend Benjamin Franklin asking, "What are you doing today?" Franklin emailed back, "Nothing. What are *you* doing today?" So Washington emailed, "Nothing. What do you want to do?" And Franklin emailed, "I don't know. What do *you* want to do?" And Washington emailed, "I asked you first."

They went back and forth like that for a while. Neither of them knew what to do, so they decided to start a new country. And that's how the United States was born.

 Arlo, you totally made that up! They didn't even *have* email in those days! The truth is, the American Revolution began because England won *another* war: the French and Indian War. The French colonists and the English colonists were fighting over who would control North America, with help from their parent countries and from Native American allies. England won, but the war cost them a lot of money, so they decided the thirteen colonies should chip in to pay for it.

 I knew that. I was just yanking your chain.

 So England started charging heavy taxes for lots of things they sold in America: sugar, coffee, newspapers, and playing cards. The colonists didn't think that was fair, because they didn't have a voice in the British Parliament. They protested. Their slogan was "No Taxation without Representation."

People started hooting and hollering and freaking out, so the British sent troops to Boston to keep them quiet. It didn't work. On March 5, 1770, the troops started shooting at an angry mob. Five colonists died. It was called the Boston Massacre. And then the people in Boston *really* freaked out.

The British pulled out their troops and got rid of all the taxes except one: a tax on tea. The colonists weren't satisfied. So one of them came up with a great idea—instead of paying the tax, they would dump the British tea into Boston Harbor!

 That was probably the first practical joke in the history of the world. The guy who came up with that idea should have gotten the No Bell Prize.*

So on December 16, 1776, a bunch of patriots dressed up as Mohawk people. They climbed aboard three British cargo ships and threw all the

* That's a prize they give to people who don't have bells.

tea overboard. It was called the Boston Tea Party.

I wonder if they dumped sugar and milk into the harbor too. Did you ever taste tea without sugar and milk? Ugh, disgusting!

To this day, nobody knows for sure who dumped the tea. The people who did it never revealed their names because they didn't want to get punished. We do know that one man named John Crane got knocked unconscious by a flying tea crate. The other patriots thought he was dead, and they hid his body under a pile of wood shavings. But the joke was on them, because Crane woke up a few hours later. Surprise!

The king of England, King George III, got *really* crazy after the Boston Tea Party. With the king's approval, Parliament closed the port, sent more soldiers, and told the colonists they had to give the soldiers food and lodging. Well, you can imagine how *that* went over with the colonists.

 Some of them got together in Philadelphia to talk about what to do next. It was called the First Continental Congress. People started to whisper about declaring independence from England and forming their own country. Isn't this exciting, Arlo?

No.

Arlo, sometimes I think you just like to disagree with everything I say no matter what it is.

 I do not.

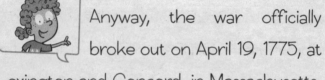 Anyway, the war officially broke out on April 19, 1775, at Lexington and Concord, in Massachusetts.

The British soldiers were called "redcoats" because their uniforms were red.

 So they had the perfect name.

 Yes, and the redcoats were planning to capture the colonists' supply of gunpowder.

 That's the powder you put into guns, so it had the perfect name too.

 Can you please stop interrupting, Arlo? Nobody cares about which things have the perfect name. Anyway, the colonists were waiting with their guns, and the redcoats were forced to retreat.

 And the colonists shouted "Nah-nah-nah boo-boo!" at them.

 Arlo, I really doubt that they shouted "Nah-nah-nah boo-boo!"

 Hey, you don't know. You weren't there.

 The next big battle was called the Battle of Bunker Hill, even though the battle *really* took place on nearby Breed's Hill.

 So it *didn't* have the perfect name.

 Shhhh! The British were planning to camp out in the hills, which were across the river from Boston. But patriot spies discovered the plan, and the night before the British were going to arrive, the patriots beat them to it, and built a fort on Breed's Hill. The British couldn't believe their eyes when they woke up the next morning.

 Ha! In their face! The patriots

must have yelled "Nah-nah-nah boo-boo!" at them then, right?

 No, but according to legend, during the battle someone yelled, "Don't shoot until you see the whites of their eyes!" After that battle, the Second Continental Congress named George Washington the commander in chief of the army. He told Congress he would take the job without pay. And he did—for eight years.

Wow, that's a long time to go without making any money. But I guess in those days they didn't have movies or video games or malls where

you could buy stuff anyway. So it probably didn't matter.

 Do you know what was one of the first things Washington did when he arrived in Massachusetts?

 Go to the bathroom? That's what I do after a long trip.

 No! He asked how much gun-powder the patriots had. When he was told that they only had thirty-six barrels, Washington was so upset that he couldn't talk for fifteen minutes. So do you know what George Washington did next?

He went to the bathroom?

 No! He sent spies into Boston to spread the rumor that they had so much gunpowder they didn't know what to do with it all. The British believed it and didn't attack.

 Ha! That gives me a good idea for a way to get out of doing homework. Just tell the teacher that you did so much homework that you didn't know what to do with it all.

 That probably won't work,

Arlo. But the patriots had to use tricks like that because they didn't have the money or supplies to defeat the British. Some of the soldiers in the Continental army had no shoes. They left bloody footprints in the snow. They couldn't afford a navy, so they hired pirates to attack British merchant ships.

 Pirates? Pirates are cool. I like when they say "Arg" all the time and dance around on peg legs with a parrot on their shoulder.

 I think that only happens with pirates on *TV*, Arlo.

Anyway, Washington faked out the British again later in the war. He let them think he was going to attack New York. He even had engineers prepare what looked like a major camp in New Jersey, complete with enough ovens to bake thousands of loaves of bread. The British got ready to defend New York. Meanwhile, Washington's army was sailing south to attack Yorktown, Virginia. That was the final battle of the war.

 Man, those British dudes would fall for *anything*.

 Here's an interesting story,

Arlo. One of the men who helped George Washington defeat the British was from France. His title was the Marquis de Lafayette. He was a major general. But the most interesting part is that when he joined the Continental army, Lafayette was just *nineteen* years old. Yes, you read that right. Nineteen! He was a *teenager.*

The Marquis de Lafayette, 1791

 I wonder if that Lafayette kid had to take time off from

school. He probably had to get permission from his parents. I can just imagine the conversation Lafayette had with his mother.

"Hey, Mom, can I go to America to help them fight their war for independence?"

"Not until you finish your homework, you can't!"

"Aw, Mom!"

"First homework, then war, young man!"

The Declaration of Independence

So the Revolutionary War had been going on for a year when the colonists decided that, gee, maybe it would be a good idea to declare that we are a separate country from England. Thomas Jefferson, from Virginia, was given the job of putting that declaration in writing.

Jefferson wrote the first draft of the Declaration of Independence, but some *other* guys helped him. And two of them were Benjamin Franklin and John Adams. All in all, eighty-six changes were made to Jefferson's first draft.

 This is the most famous sentence in the Declaration of Independence: *We hold these truths to be self-evident, that all men are created equal, that they are endowed by their Creator with certain unalienable Rights, that*

among these are Life, Liberty and the pursuit of Happiness.

 By the way, the word "independence" never appears in the Declaration of Independence.

 Signing the declaration was *dangerous*. The signers were committing treason against their king and the British government. Treason was a crime punishable by death! In fact, Benjamin Franklin told the group, "We must all hang together, or assuredly we shall all

Benjamin Franklin

hang separately."

Ben Franklin was a riot. I bet he was a lot of fun at parties.

Here's a good question to ask your parents: How many of the men who signed the Declaration of Independence were born in the United States?

The answer: *none* of them! They *couldn't* have been born in the United States because the United States didn't exist as a country until they signed the Declaration! Ha! In fact, the first time the words "United States of America" appeared, it was in the Declaration of Independence.

The *first* person to sign the Declaration was John Hancock, because he was the president of the Continental Congress. He wrote his name really big, almost five inches wide. Because of that, his name became part of the language. If you ever hear somebody say, "Put your John Hancock here," it means to sign your name there.

Benjamin Franklin was seventy years old, and he was the oldest person to sign the Declaration. The two youngest signers were Thomas Lynch Jr. and

Edward Rutledge. Both of them were twenty-six, and both were from South Carolina. Twenty-four of the fifty-six signers were lawyers. And all the signers were men. Not a single woman signed the Declaration. That's not fair!*

 Two future presidents signed the Declaration: John Adams and Thomas Jefferson.

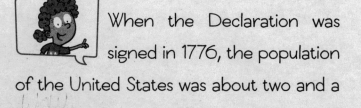 When the Declaration was signed in 1776, the population of the United States was about two and a

---

* Women wouldn't even be allowed to vote for another 144 years!

half million people. Today it's over 323 million!

 Two hundred copies of the Declaration were printed. Only twenty-six of them are still around. If you find one, hang onto it! In 1989, a guy bought an old picture frame for four dollars at a flea market in Pennsylvania. And you'll never believe in a million hundred years what he found behind the picture—one of those two hundred Declarations! Wow! The TV producer Norman Lear bought it for more than eight million dollars!

The original signed parchment copy of the Declaration is at the National Archives Building in Washington, DC. You can go see it there. It has only left the capital twice. The first time was when the British attacked Washington during the War of 1812. The second time was during World War II.

 In the 2004 movie *National Treasure*, a guy has to steal the Declaration so he can read a secret message written on the back of it. There actually *is* writing on the back, but it's no secret message. It just says "Original Declaration of Independence dated 4th July 1776."

Speaking of the Fourth of July, one of our presidents was born on that date—Calvin Coolidge. And here's an amazing coincidence: two of the Founding Fathers—Thomas Jefferson and John Adams—both died on the Fourth of July in 1826! And that was exactly fifty years after the first Independence Day.

 That's weird!

 Here's the weird thing. We celebrate the Fourth of July as our Independence Day, but the Declaration of Independence wasn't signed on July 4.

What?! You mean the Fourth of July is bogus?

 Calm down, Arlo! Here's what really happened: On July 2, the Second Continental Congress met in Philadelphia and voted in favor of independence. They spent the next two days revising Thomas Jefferson's draft. On July 4, they officially adopted the Declaration. But they didn't sign it that day. Most of the delegates signed it on August 2. Two of them, John Dickinson and Robert R. Livingston, never signed at *all*.

On July 9, George Washington read the Declaration out loud in front of City Hall. The cheering crowd got so riled up that they tore down a nearby statue of King George III. And do you know what they did with it? They melted it down and made it into more than forty-two thousand musket balls for the American army.

It must have helped. After seven years of bloody fighting, the British finally surrendered, and the United States of America was a free and independent country. Yay!

 I knew all that.

 You did not!

Chapter 5

The Constitution

 Here's a little quiz, Arlo. After the United States declared our independence and won the Revolutionary War, what did we need to do next?

 Go to the bathroom? That war lasted *years*. We must have been holding it in for a long time.

No, Arlo! We needed a constitution! I bet you don't even know that a constitution is the system of values and laws that's used to govern a country.

 I knew that. In fact, I even know that our *first* constitution, back in 1781, was called the Articles of Confederation. But that was when the United States was just a bunch of unconnected states. In 1786,

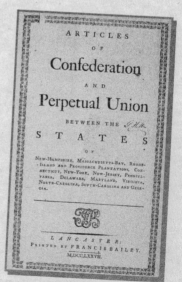

Articles of Confederation

Alexander Hamilton called for a meeting in Philadelphia, where they decided to write a *new* constitution that would tie all the states together.

 Wow, I'm impressed! I thought you only cared about video games and skateboarding.

I remember this stuff by imagining the Founding Fathers skateboarding and playing video games while they were writing the Constitution.

 Actually, the Constitution was written in the same building in Philadelphia where the Declaration of Independence was signed, and the building is still there today. It's called Independence Hall. Twelve of the thirteen states sent representatives to work on the Constitution. The only state that didn't send anyone was Rhode Island.

 I guess they had something more important to do that day.

Actually, it was because they didn't want a powerful national government meddling in their business.

 That too. And the whole thing was top secret. They wrote the Constitution behind locked doors that were guarded by sentries.

 Do you know who was chosen to be the president of the convention, Arlo?

 Chuck Norris?

George Washington

No, dumbhead! It was George Washington!

 I knew that too. It took the whole summer of 1787 to write the Constitution. And after all that, it's only four pages long. That's just one page a month! But it was a really important document, so they wanted to get it right. It's the oldest—and shortest—constitution of any major government in the world.

 The Constitution has forty-four hundred words in it. I counted! That's about half as long as a My Weird School book.

My Weird School books have a great opening. They all start with the words "My name is A.J. and I hate . . ." What does the Constitution start with?

 "We the People."

Well, that's pretty good too.

Believe it or not, after all that careful work, there are

spelling errors in the Constitution! The most obvious one is right above the signers' names. A delegate from Pennsylvania spelled his own state Pensylvania!

 Boy, that guy must have been a real dumbhead! He couldn't even spell his own state.

 Pennsylvania must be really hard for people to spell. It's also misspelled on the Liberty Bell.

 Too bad they didn't have spell-check in those days.

While they were writing the Constitution, they had a lot of arguments. Kind of like us, huh?

 Yeah. One of the biggest fights they had was over slavery. Some of the states wanted to get rid of it. Other states wanted to keep it. In the end, to hold the country together, they agreed to let slavery continue. But that didn't exactly end the argument, because seventy-four years later we fought a Civil War over the same issue.

 Finally, on September 17, 1787, the Constitution was finished

and it was ready to be signed. Thirty-nine men (yes, they were all men, of course!) signed it. George Washington and James Madison were the only presidents who signed the Constitution. Thomas Jefferson and John Adams never signed it. Do you know why?

Because they were in the bathroom?

 No, Arlo! They were in other countries! Thomas Jefferson was representing the United States in France and John Adams was doing the same thing in England.

 Maybe they were going to the bathroom in other countries.

 What is it with you and bathrooms, Arlo? Bathrooms have nothing to do with the history of the United States.

That's where you're wrong, Andrea. You'll see what I mean in Chapter 13.

 What's in Chapter 13?

 Oh, you'll find out.

 Did you know that the youngest signer of the Constitution was Jonathan Dayton of New Jersey? He was just twenty-six. The oldest signer was eighty-one-year-old Benjamin Franklin. He could hardly walk, so he was carried into the convention hall every day in a sedan chair by prisoners from the local jail. That's true! And when Franklin was signing the Constitution, he got so emotional that tears were streaming down his face.

 Either that, or they were cutting onions in the next room.

 I think I should just ignore you. Only six people signed both the Declaration of Independence *and* the Constitution. They were Benjamin Franklin, George Read, Roger Sherman, Robert Morris, George Clymer, and James Wilson.

When the Constitutional Convention was over, Benjamin Franklin pointed at the symbol of a half-sun on George Washington's chair. He said, "I have the happiness to know that it is a rising and not a setting sun."

 Speaking of George Washington, he was the guy who formally established the first Thanksgiving in 1789. It had nothing to do with

Pilgrims or Native Americans or turkeys. The reason for the new holiday was to give thanks for the new Constitution.

Nobody's Perfect!

 The Constitution wasn't perfect, of course. *Nothing's* perfect. Well, except for me, of course. But the Founding Fathers knew the world was going to change, and they were smart enough to know they should let future generations make changes in the Constitution.

Over eleven thousand changes—or amendments—

have been introduced in Congress. Only twenty-seven of them have been approved. The first ten became known as the Bill of Rights.

The Thirteenth Amendment abolished slavery.

The Nineteenth Amendment gave women the right to vote.

 The Twenty-Eighth Amendment gives kids the right to stay home from school whenever they feel like it.

Well, that last one hasn't been ratified yet. But it should be!

A Few Founding Fathers Fast Facts

 The Founding Fathers weren't just a bunch of old farts you see on dollar bills and coins. They were real people who worked together to create the United States of America. But I'll bet you didn't know that John Adams was over-weight, and people called him "His Rotundity."*

 He was the first president to live in the White House too. But he lost his bid for reelection and had to move out four months later.

 Ben Franklin invented swim fins. That's right! When he was

---

* He should have gone on Weight Watchers. It worked for my mom.

a kid, he attached wooden planks to his hands and feet to help him swim faster!

 Not only that, but he also used to sit around with no clothes on. That's not a joke! Most mornings, before he began work, Franklin took what he called an "air bath." He'd sit around naked! Hmmm, I wonder if he wore his swim fins.

James Madison's face is on the five-thousand-dollar bill. That's right, there's a five-thousand-dollar bill! Can you imagine going into a store to buy a candy bar and asking if they'll give you change for a five-thousand-dollar bill?

 George Washington was rich in land but not in money. When he became president of the United States, he had to borrow money from a friend to make the trip to New York City for his inauguration!

Washington also bred hunting dogs, and he gave them names like Tartar, Truelove, Sweet Lips, Drunkard, and Tipsy.

And then there's Thomas Jefferson. He was the first president who had a pet that lived in the White House: Dick, a mockingbird. Dick would sit on Jefferson's shoulder as he worked in his office. Jefferson would also put food between his lips and let Dick swoop down and take it.

When Jefferson took out his violin and started playing, Dick would sing along. That was just weird.

 Jefferson wrote this inscription for his own gravestone: "Here was buried Thomas Jefferson, Author of the Declaration of American Independence, of the Statute of Virginia for religious freedom & Father of the University of Virginia." The weird thing is that he never mentioned he was also president of the United States!

 Jefferson had some forty-million-year-old mastodon bones

sent to him at the White House. He laid the bones out in the East Room and tried to build a skeleton out of them.

 The Founding Fathers were weird.

It's Getting Bigger!

 North America is *big*. Almost as soon as our country was born, people realized it was a very cool place, and they wanted to spread across the continent. In 1803, President Thomas Jefferson *doubled* the size of America with one stroke of a pen when he bought the Louisiana Territory from France. It cost fifteen million dollars! That's a *lot* of money. But look what he got for it—the area that's now Arkansas, Missouri, Iowa, Oklahoma, Kansas, Nebraska, and parts of Minnesota, North Dakota, South Dakota, New Mexico, Texas, Montana, Wyoming, Colorado, and Louisiana!

 The funny thing is, Jefferson had no idea what he'd paid for! It was like when you buy a pack of baseball cards and you don't know which cards you got until you open it up. So Jefferson sent two explorers, Meriwether Lewis and William Clark, to find out what he'd bought. On May 14, 1804, Lewis and

Clark left St. Louis, Missouri, and headed west. It wasn't easy. Remember, there were no hotels back then. They slept outside. There were no restaurants along the way where they could stop and eat. There were no roads or highways. No nothing! Lewis and Clark were exploring the wilderness.

But then they got lucky. In November, in what we now call North Dakota, they met a Native American woman named Sacagawea. She joined the expedition, traveling thousands of miles while carrying her newborn son on her back. Sacagawea served as Lewis and Clark's guide, interpreter, and

negotiator. Who knows what might have happened to them if she hadn't been around to help out?

 Finally, in November 1805, the expedition reached the Pacific Ocean and headed east again. They didn't make it back to Sacagawea's village until

August 1806. And do you know how much she was paid for all the work she'd done?

Nothing! And she didn't get any frequent flyer miles either. Totally not fair!

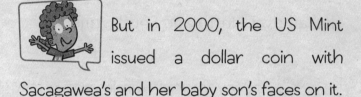 But in 2000, the US Mint issued a dollar coin with Sacagawea's and her baby son's faces on it.

 A lot of good that did her. She died in 1812.

Immigration

 If you live in the United States, somebody in your family was an immigrant. We're *all* immigrants!

Maybe your distant relatives walked over a land bridge from Asia to Alaska during the last ice age. When the ice melted, the land bridge disappeared, and those immigrants settled all over North and South America.

 Maybe your family arrived in New England from England during the first Great Migration (1630–1640), or maybe they lived in one of the original thirteen colonies.

 Maybe they came from Italy, Sweden, or Germany. Maybe they came from France and settled in

Louisiana, or they ran away from Ireland during the Irish Potato Famine in the 1840s.

 Maybe they came from China during the 1849 California gold rush. Hardly any of them found gold, but they became farmers or fishermen, or they built the railroads or opened up a laundry. Maybe they came from Poland or Russia, Central America or Spain.

 People came to the United States from all over the world for lots of reasons. They were poor and hungry. They wanted to practice their religion freely, or they wanted to be free to speak their minds. People in other countries were hearing about America and this new form of government where people could vote for their own leaders. They wanted to come here too. Waves of immigrants started arriving from all over the world. They all hoped for freedom, opportunity, and a better life.

 From 1840 to 1940, nearly forty *million* immigrants arrived in the United States, most sailing past the Statue of Liberty and through the processing center

The Statue of Liberty was a symbol of hope for many immigrants coming to America.

at Ellis Island. America became a nation of immigrants, and that made us who we are as a country.

 It wasn't easy being a poor immigrant coming to America. Many people came over in big, slow ships and had to stay in a dark room in the bottom of the ship. A hundred and fifty people would be crowded together with very little food, and not enough fresh water to drink and wash. They had to use a bucket in the corner for a bathroom. Yuck! And they had to live like that for the month or so it took to get here.

New immigrants had to pass lots of tests to enter the United States. Parents had to be healthy and able to work. One examination everyone hated was the one to make sure they didn't have contagious eye infections. Examiners turned people's eyelids inside out with small metal hooks. Ouch!

 People who were sick got chalk

marks on their backs. If there was no cure for their illness, they would be sent back where they came from.

 And of course, one large group of people came here because they had no choice. They were thrown onto ships in Africa and *forced* to go to America to become slaves. In 1680, there were about seven thousand African

slaves in America. By 1790, there were seven hundred thousand. They had the hardest time of all.

I can't even make any jokes about that. It just isn't funny.

Chapter 8

Rise of the Machines!

All those people coming to America needed to find work. And it just so happened there was plenty of work to do, thanks to this little thing that started in the 1800s called the Industrial Revolution. It was all about machines.

101

You mean like toilets?

 No, Arlo! Not like toilets! Here's the thing—before the Industrial Revolution, most people lived on farms, and when they needed something, they made it themselves, by hand. But when machines were invented, things could be mass-produced in factories, and people moved to cities where the factories and jobs were. Take clothes, for instance. Everybody needs clothes, right?

 Even Neil the nude kid needs clothes.

Right. Before the Industrial Revolution, people made their clothes at home, and most clothes were made from cotton. But cotton was expensive to use, because it was filled with these tiny black seeds that had to be picked out one by one. That is, until this guy from Massachusetts named Eli Whitney invented the cotton gin in 1794.

He made gin? Isn't that a drink?

 No, gin is short for "engine." Instead of cleaning one pound of cotton in a day, with a cotton gin you could clean *fifty* pounds.

 And this British guy named Samuel Slater built a cotton-spinning mill next to a river in Pawtucket, Rhode Island. Slater's mill used the force of flowing water to power the machinery. It was the first factory in the United States, and it was a big success. There are tons of rivers in New England, so mills popped up everywhere. Soon there were lots more clothes to buy, and they were cheaper because machines were used to make the cloth.

Farming improved too. In 1831, Cyrus McCormick from Virginia invented a mechanical reaper, and farmers didn't have to cut wheat by hand anymore. They could harvest it much faster. Factories could produce more food.

The only problem was that all these factories had to be next to rivers. That is, until the steam engine came along! This guy from Scotland named James Watt built a machine that could burn coal, which boiled water and created steam. The steam engine could power factories *anywhere*. Not only that, but it could power locomotives and ships.

Steam locomotive

Watt's steam engine

 America was on the move! Wasn't the Industrial Revolution wonderful, Arlo?

Well, yeah, if you don't mention that factories led to the rise of sweatshops. Do you know what a sweatshop is? It's a factory that makes sweat, so it has the perfect name. Yuck!

 Sweatshops didn't make sweat, dumbhead! They were factories where people had to work long hours in tiny, noisy, dirty rooms, sometimes with no windows.

 I knew that. It sounds horrible.

 It was. And people lived in overcrowded apartments.

107

There was pollution from burning all that coal. Diseases spread easily.

 Don't forget about the rats. Newspapers were full of rat stories, and reports of rats as big as dogs. Gross! But here's the *worst* part. They had *kids* working in a lot of those factories! In 1820, half of the industrial workers in the United States were children under the age of ten. Some of them worked twelve-hour days, six days a week. Some of the jobs involved

working with dangerous machines. And they hardly earned any money at all. It wasn't until 1938 that laws went into effect so that kids couldn't work in factories.

Children at the "Kindergarten Factory" in High Point, NC, 1912

Here's a cute story, Arlo. Single women who worked in factories had a hard time finding husbands. So they started hiding notes in the men's clothing they were making. They wrote things like "I hope you will be well pleased with this hat. If you have a few minutes' time, please write and tell me how you like your hat. Of course you must be a single man, as I am a single girl." It was like a dating service. At one factory in Pennsylvania, twelve women found husbands this way!*

 The Industrial Revolution created a lot of jobs, but it also took *away* a lot of jobs. Machines could do things that people used to do (or in some cases, horses and mules used to do). Some craftsmen saw their jobs wiped out by the new machines.

---

* Hmmm, maybe I'll start leaving little notes in Arlo's clothes.

Did you ever hear of the Luddites, Arlo?

 Of course. Everybody knows about the Luddites. I know everything there is to know about the Luddites.

 Who were the Luddites, Arlo?

 Uh, they were this group of people . . .

 Yes?

And they did this thing . . .

 Arlo, you have no idea who the Luddites were, do you?

 No clue.

 The Luddites were a group of English workers who were really angry about machines taking over their jobs. This was around 1811 to 1817. So they protested, rioted, and even destroyed some of the machines. That wasn't very nice. These days, if someone doesn't like new technology, sometimes they're called a Luddite.

 Well, it didn't matter what those Luddites did. The world was changing as new and better machines were developed. This guy named Elisha Otis invented the elevator, and the next thing anybody knew skyscrapers were popping up everywhere. Thomas Edison invented the lightbulb and lit up the world. Both good and bad things happened as a result of the Industrial Revolution. You can't hold back the future.

Chapter 9

The Civil War

 It's sad, but wars are a big part of history. From 1861 to 1865, our country fought one of the bloodiest wars ever. The amazing thing was that we didn't even fight against another country. We fought a war against *ourselves*. It was the Civil War.

It's complicated, but it pretty much

boiled down to some of the states (the South, or "the Confederacy") wanting to keep slavery and some of the states (the North, or "the Union") wanting to get rid of it. The Union won the Civil War, and it changed America in many ways.

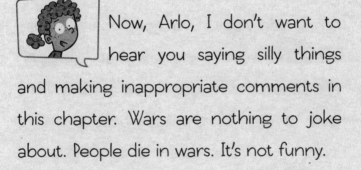 Now, Arlo, I don't want to hear you saying silly things and making inappropriate comments in this chapter. Wars are nothing to joke about. People die in wars. It's not funny.

 Chill, Andrea. Don't worry. I won't say anything rude. Toilets!

You're impossible! Anyway, here are some weird fast facts about the Civil War. I'll go first. . . .

The first shots of the Civil War were fired at Fort Sumter, South Carolina, on April 12, 1861. On one side was Confederate general P. G. T. Beauregard. On the other side was U.S. major Robert Anderson. The weird thing was that Anderson was Beauregard's teacher when they were both at West Point military academy!

 General Stonewall Jackson was injured in the Battle of Chancellorsville and had to have one of his arms amputated. The arm got a proper burial,

complete with a head-
stone. When Jackson
eventually died, he was
buried over a hundred
miles away from his arm.
So I guess you could say
that he rests in pieces.

Get it? Rest in peace? Rest in pieces?
That's a joke!

 The man's arm was cut off,
Arlo! That's nothing to joke
about!

 Okay, okay. How about this?
In 1862, a Virginia farmer

gave Confederate General Robert E. Lee a flock of chickens. His men ate all the chickens except one, who survived by making her roost in a tree overhanging Lee's tent. Lee decided that he liked the chicken. He named her Nellie, and she was allowed to go in and out of his tent as she pleased. Then one day Lee invited some other generals to have dinner with him, but his cook couldn't find enough food to make a meal. So he cooked Nellie! It was the only time in four years that Lee yelled at his cook.

During the war, General Lee's Virginia estate was confiscated by the Union and turned into a cemetery. Today, that cemetery is called Arlington National Cemetery. Four hundred thousand people are buried there, including Presidents William H. Taft and John F. Kennedy.

 After the Battle of Shiloh,

soldiers on both sides noticed that their wounds glowed in the dark. That must have been weird! As a matter of fact, the glow-in-the-dark wounds seemed to heal better than the others. This mystery wasn't solved until 2001, when two Maryland teenagers figured out that the wounded men became hypothermic, and their lowered body temperatures made for perfect living conditions for a bacteria that glows in the dark.

 Abraham Lincoln is remembered as one of our greatest presidents, but he never thought he would become president. When he was running for the Senate in 1858, Lincoln's wife told him she was convinced he would be president one day. Lincoln told a reporter, "Just think of such a sucker as me as president!"

Lincoln's Gettysburg Address, one of the most famous speeches in history, was considered a failure by Lincoln himself when he made it. In those days speeches could last for hours. In fact, Edward Everett, the speaker just before Lincoln, droned on for two hours. Lincoln's speech was so short—about two minutes—that it was over before many people even knew he had begun. The photographers didn't even have time to set up their cameras. That's why there's no photograph of Lincoln delivering the Gettysburg Address.

 You may know that President Lincoln was assassinated just five days after the Civil War ended. But you probably don't know that he was also shot two years *earlier.* In August 1864, Lincoln was riding a horse by himself when a shot rang out. It didn't hit the president, but the bullet went right through his hat. The pres- ident asked his guards to keep the story

quiet. He didn't want to worry his wife, Mary.

 The Union army didn't have enough men to fight the war, so Congress started to draft soldiers. Any man between the ages of twenty and forty-five had to register. The weird thing was, you could buy your way out of the army by paying three hundred dollars. That wasn't fair.

 You probably think that the soldiers in the Civil War were all men. In fact, hundreds of women on both sides pretended to *be* men so they could join the army. Some of them did it for adventure, but many did it for the money. Union soldiers got paid about thirteen dollars a month. That's close to double what a woman could make at the time.

 The airplane hadn't been invented during the Civil War. But both the Union army and the Confederate army did use hot-air balloons to spot enemy soldiers and coordinate troop movements.

 They also had subs.

Sub sandwiches? Yum!

 No, Arlo.

 Substitute teachers?

 No. Submarines! The Union army had a paddle-powered submarine called the *Alligator.* They thought they would use it to attack ships, but the *Alligator* got caught in bad weather and sank before it ever saw combat. It's still below the ocean somewhere. Nobody knows where.

A few months after the *Alligator* sank, the Confederates launched a submarine of their own, the *H.L. Hunley*. It was more successful. It sank the USS *Housatonic* off the coast of Charleston, making it the first submarine ever to sink an enemy ship. The only problem is that not long afterward the *H.L. Hunley* also sank, and all eight crewmen drowned.

During the war, Southerners were proud of the sacrifices they made. They invited each other to "starvation parties." Do you know what was served at a starvation party? Nothing! No food! So starvation parties had the perfect name.

Paul Revere's grandson fought and died in the Battle of Gettysburg. On July 2, 1863, he was wounded by a shell fragment that pierced his lung, and he died two days later.

 Baseball was invented before the Civil War, but many Union and Confederate soldiers played the game for the first time while they were serving in the army. When the war was over, they came home and brought the game of baseball with them. That's how it spread across the country.

 About 625,000 men died in the Civil War. That's more

than the number of deaths in World War I, World War II, the Korean War, and the Vietnam War *combined*. Many of the soldiers were killed by bullets or cannon fire. But do you know what killed more of them than anything else? Disease! Medical care was very primitive in the 1860s, and battlefields became breeding grounds for mumps, chicken pox, measles, and infections. A million Union soldiers got malaria, and epidemics were common. These are not things we should joke about.

Chapter 10

The World Wars

World War I

At the beginning of the 20th century, Europe was basically two large families. The Allies—the British Empire, France, and Russia—were in one family. The Central Powers—Germany, Austria-Hungary, Bulgaria, and Turkey—were another family. Then, on June 28,

1914, Archduke Franz Ferdinand, the heir to the Austro-Hungarian throne, was assassinated by a Serbian nationalist. Austria-Hungary declared war on Serbia. Russia was allied to Serbia. Germany declared war on Russia and its ally France. Great Britain declared war on Germany.

 Wait a minute. What does that have to do with America?

 Well, the United States tried to stay out of the war, but in 1915 Germany began to attack and sink American ships in the Atlantic Ocean. President Woodrow Wilson asked Congress to declare war on Germany. And

President Woodrow Wilson

the next thing anybody knew, the whole world was at war. Arlo, maybe you can dig up some weird fast facts about World War I.

Way ahead of you, Andrea. Here they are. . . .

• Worms helped us win the war. No kidding! Soldiers collected glowworms in jars to help them see at night. The worms gave off enough light to read and write letters, but not so much as to attract enemy fire.

- Garden slugs also helped us win the war. When slugs detect poisonous mustard gas, they curl up to protect themselves. Whenever that happened, soldiers knew to put on their gas masks quickly.

- Pigeons helped us win the war! They were used to carry small capsules with messages, maps, photos, and even tiny cameras to the front lines and back. About a hundred thousand homing pigeons "fought" in World War I. One pigeon named Cher Ami saved five hundred American soldiers by delivering a vital message from the soldiers who had been cut off behind enemy lines. He was shot and blinded in one eye, and he lost a leg, but army doctors saved his life and gave him a wooden leg. He was awarded a medal for bravery!

• Frankfurt is a city in Germany. But Americans were so angry at Germany that during the war they changed the name of frankfurters to "liberty sausages." Sauerkraut became "liberty cabbage." Dachshunds became "liberty dogs." And the Statue of Liberty became . . . well, she just stayed the way she always was.

• If it hadn't been for World War I, we may have never had plastic surgery!

So many soldiers came home from that war with their faces messed up from combat that a doctor named Harold Gillies developed techniques to repair their injuries. He became known as "the father of modern plastic surgery."

- The youngest soldier in the war was a twelve-year-old British boy named Sidney Lewis. He lied about his age and joined the army. Sidney was one of 250,000 boys who fought in the war.

- On Christmas Day 1914, both sides agreed to a cease-fire near Ypres, Belgium. During the truce, some German and British troops played a game of soccer against each other in the middle of the two armies, the area called "no-man's-land." When the game was over, everybody went back to shooting at each other again. Germany won the game, but lost the war.

- Finally, World War I ended in 1918, at the eleventh hour on the eleventh day of the eleventh month. *Weird*.

World War II

 Just about twenty years after World War I ended, the world exploded into *another* war, even more bloody than the last one! This time, the cause was primarily one madman, Adolf Hitler, who became the leader of Germany in 1933 and decided that Germany should rule the world. Japan and Italy joined him in 1940. England fought back, and after the United States was attacked at Pearl Harbor in Hawaii, America joined the British and entered the war. It lasted until

Adolf Hitler

1945, when we dropped atomic bombs on Japan. I'm sure Arlo has some weird fast facts about World War II that he'd like to share.

 I sure do! Here's the best one: Adolf Hitler's nephew, William Hitler, served in the U.S. Navy during the war!

That's not a joke. He was even wounded in battle and won the Purple Heart. You can look it up if you don't believe me. Can you imagine going through life in America with the name Hitler? I guess that's why William changed his name to William Stuart-Houston after the war was over. He became a businessman in New York and died in 1987.

On December 7, 1941, the day America was attacked at Pearl Harbor, the Secret Service realized they didn't have a car with bulletproof windows to protect President Franklin D. Roosevelt. Legend has it, a Secret Service agent remembered that the notorious gangster Al Capone had a bulletproof car, and it had been confiscated when he was arrested in 1931. The car still worked, so the president rode in Al Capone's car on his way to make his famous Pearl Harbor speech. An hour later, Congress declared war on Japan.

President Roosevelt delivering his famous Pearl Harbor speech

Okay, are you ready for this? During World War II, British soldiers were only given *three* sheets of toilet paper a day!

Three sheets! That's *it*! American soldiers got twenty-two sheets.

 Arlo, I thought you were going to wait until Chapter 13 to talk about toilet stuff.

 I couldn't resist.

Nobody is sure who really invented the hamburger, but some historians say it was named after the city of Hamburg, Germany.* During the war, some Americans ate "liberty steaks" instead of "hamburgers."

---

* Yes, Germany has a Frankfurt and a Hamburg. I wonder if there's a city in France called French Fries.

I wonder if they changed the name of German shepherds to "liberty dogs."

 They *didn't*. In fact, a German shepherd mix named Chips was a hero dog during World War II. When Italian soldiers started shooting at him and his human handler, Chips attacked them, biting and barking until they surrendered. Chips was wounded, and he was awarded a Silver Star and a Purple Heart.

Even though radio technology had improved since the last World War, the United States Army still used pigeons in World War II. A special cage and parachute were developed to drop pigeons from airplanes to isolated troops. Thousands of pigeons were dropped over France, and French people used them to send back information about German troop movements.

When US troops stormed the beaches of Normandy, France, on June 6, 1944 (D-day), the mission was so secret that the Allies communicated *only* through pigeons. One bird named Gustav flew more than 150 miles from Normandy to England to deliver the news.

But the most famous pigeon of the war

was GI Joe. On October 18, 1943, the plan was to bomb the German-occupied town of Calvi Vecchia in Italy. But then the Germans retreated from the town and British troops moved in just before the bombing was about to begin. The British couldn't cancel the attack by radio. With time running out, GI Joe was sent with the message to cancel the bombing. He flew twenty miles in twenty minutes and arrived just as bombers were about to take off. He saved about a thousand lives.

It must have been easy to spot airplanes sitting on the ground, and to bomb them,

GI Joe with PDSA Dickin Medal for Valor

right? That's why the army decided to disguise the Lockheed Burbank Aircraft Plant in California. They hired artists from nearby film studios such as Disney to make the plant look like an ordinary California suburb from above! Airfields were painted green and lined with plants to make them look like alfalfa fields. The main factory was covered with a painted canvas to blend in with the surrounding grass. Finally, fake trees were put up with spray-painted chicken feathers for leaves.

Do you know how some captured soldiers escaped from German prison camps? They used the game Monopoly! It's

Lockheed Burbank Aircraft Plant

true! The Red Cross sent packages to prisoners, and one of the things that could be included were board games. So special Monopoly boxes were made that contained items to help the prisoners escape: Real money was hidden within the Monopoly money. A metal file was hidden within the board. A small compass was hidden in a play piece. Maps of the prison and its location were hidden inside the hotel pieces. That is cool.

Native Americans haven't been treated very well in America, but they have fought bravely for it. Thousands of them joined the military to fight in World War I even though Native Americans were not all granted citizenship until six years after the war was over.

And during World War II, a group of Navajo devised a code using their native language that made it possible to send and receive secret messages. They were called Code Talkers. The Japanese were never able to break their code.

When the war ended, some Japanese soldiers were hiding in the jungles of the Philippines. They didn't know the war was over. One of them, Hiroo Onoda, didn't surrender or leave his post until 1974. That was almost *thirty* years after the war was over!

Russia and Japan have never signed an official peace treaty with each other to end World War II. Both countries are still disputing who owns the Kuril Islands.

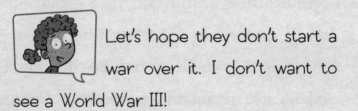 Let's hope they don't start a war over it. I don't want to see a World War III!

Chapter 11

Weird Fast Facts about the Presidents

Arlo, let's take turns sharing weird facts about the presidents!

Okay, I go first. By the time he became president, George

Washington had only one real tooth left in his mouth. His false teeth were made from hippopotamus, walrus, and elephant ivory, and cow, elk, and human teeth.

 In 1807, the explorer Zebulon Pike sent Thomas Jefferson two grizzly bear cubs. They lived in a cage on the White House lawn.

 At James Madison's second inaugural ball, his wife, Dolley, served a special treat—ice cream! Most people had never tasted it before. The First Lady's favorite flavor was oyster. Yuck! Gross! Madison was the smallest president, by the way. He was only about five feet, four inches tall and weighed less than a hundred pounds. What a shrimp!

 During the Revolutionary War, James Monroe was wounded at the Battle of Trenton. He carried a bullet in his shoulder for the rest of his life. He died on the Fourth of July, just like John Adams and Thomas Jefferson, but five years later.

John Quincy Adams used to go swimming in the Potomac River—naked! One time, someone stole his clothes while Adams was swimming.

He had to ask a boy to go to the White House and get him something to wear.

For his inauguration party, twenty thousand citizens stormed the White House to greet Andrew Jackson. Things got out of control, so he sneaked out a window and went to a hotel. The people wouldn't leave the White House, so tubs of punch were put out on the front lawn. When the partygoers went outside to drink, the White House staff locked the doors and windows so the people couldn't come back.

According to legend, the word "okay" was invented when Martin Van Buren was running for reelection in 1840. He was from Old Kinderhook, New York, and his nickname was "Old Kinderhook." While he was campaigning for president, people shortened it to "O.K."

William Henry Harrison's inaugural address was 8,445 words long. That's longer than a My Weird School book! It took Harrison about two hours to read it, and he did it on a cold, wet day, with no coat or hat. And do you know what happened a month later? Harrison died of pneumonia! So he had the longest speech and the shortest term of any president.

 Zachary Taylor was the *second* president to die in office. He celebrated the Fourth of July in 1850 at the Washington Monument. It was a hot day, and Taylor cooled off with buttermilk and cherries that were probably contaminated with bacteria. He got sick and died five days later.

John Tyler had more children than any other president: fifteen! His last child was born when he was seventy years old.

 Abraham Lincoln used to store his mail, his bankbook, and important papers in his stovepipe hat. I guess they didn't have briefcases in those days.

 Ulysses S. Grant was once pulled over for speeding in Washington, DC, and he didn't even have a car! The police officer took away Grant's horse and carriage, and the president had to walk the rest of the way home to the White House. He paid a twenty-dollar speeding ticket.

 Rutherford B. Hayes was the first president to have a telephone in the White House. Alexander Graham Bell, the inventor of the telephone, installed it himself. Do you want to know what the president's phone number was? It was *1*.

 James A. Garfield didn't think people should get appointed to important posts in the government just because they knew the president. One man was angry when Garfield refused to give him a job, so he shot the president. Garfield died eleven weeks later. But it wasn't the bullet that killed him. The operations to remove the bullet with dirty instruments led to blood poisoning that really killed the president.

 Chester A. Arthur was nicknamed Elegant Arthur in the press because he liked nice clothes. Arthur owned eighty pairs of pants. That's a lot of pants! By the way, do you know why golfers always carry two pairs of pants? They might get a hole in one. That's a joke!

Benjamin Harrison was so formal that the White House staff secretly called him "The Human Iceberg." He was also the first president to have electricity in the White House. First Lady Caroline Lavinia Harrison was afraid to touch the light switches, so she never turned them on.

 William McKinley was the first president to ride in this new invention called the automobile. But it wasn't much fun for McKinley. He got the ride in an ambulance after he was shot and rushed to the hospital.

Teddy Roosevelt went on a bear hunt in 1902, but there was one problem—there were no bears! His guide finally found an old bear and tied it to a tree so Roosevelt could shoot it. But the president refused. A store owner in Brooklyn, New York, heard the story and asked his wife to create a stuffed bear. He put it in his store window with a sign that read TEDDY'S BEAR. And that's how the teddy bear was born.

 William Taft was the largest president ever. He weighed 332 pounds. He was so big, a custom-made tub was built just for Taft. It was big enough for four regular-size men. That is, if four regular-size men took a bath together.

When the United States entered World War I, President Woodrow Wilson brought a flock of sheep to the White House. The sheep "mowed" the lawn, which saved gas and labor. Their wool was auctioned to earn money for the Red Cross and for war hospitals.

Warren G. Harding had the biggest feet of any president—size 14!

Calvin Coolidge didn't talk much, and he was nicknamed Silent Cal. One time, a dinner guest told him she made a bet that she could get him to say more than three words. The president replied, "You lose."

Franklin D. Roosevelt was afraid of the number thirteen. If there were thirteen people at dinner, FDR would invite his secretary to join the group to make it an even fourteen. He would never leave for a trip on the thirteenth of the month. People who are afraid of the number thirteen have what is called "triskaidekaphobia."

Alaska and Hawaii joined the United States during the presidency of Dwight D. Eisenhower, who was also called Ike. At the end of his time in office, people chanted, "Ike is nifty, Ike is nifty; started out with forty-eight; ended up with fifty."

Major General Eisenhower, eleven years before he was elected president

There are some curious coincidences between Abraham Lincoln and John F. Kennedy. They were elected exactly a hundred years apart, Lincoln in 1860 and Kennedy in 1960. Lincoln's secretary was named Kennedy. Kennedy's secretary was named Lincoln. Both men were assassinated. And both of their vice presidents—named Johnson—became president.

 Do you know why Lyndon B. Johnson and his wife, Lady Bird Johnson, named their daughters Lynda Bird and Luci Baines? They did it so that all four members of the family would have the initials LBJ.

Richard Nixon liked bowling

so much that he had a bowling alley installed in the White House.

 Gerald R. Ford helped pay for law school by working as a fashion model. He was once on the cover of *Cosmopolitan* magazine.

Jimmy Carter grew up on a peanut farm in Georgia and sold boiled peanuts from a wagon by the side of the road. He was the first

American president to be born in a hospital. Before Carter, all the other presidents were born at home.

 Before becoming president, Ronald Reagan was a popular movie actor. One of his most famous films was the 1951 comedy *Bedtime for Bonzo*. Reagan played a college professor who has to raise a chimpanzee as if it was a human baby.

Here's a trivia question for you: Who was the only president in history to throw up on a foreign dignitary? It was George H. W. Bush. In 1992, he was at a banquet at the home of the prime minister of Japan. Suddenly, Bush turned around and vomited in the prime minister's lap! That was weird! Afterward, the Japanese used the term *Bushu-suru* for throwing up. It means "to do the Bush thing."

 Bill Clinton is one of the few presidents who won a Grammy

164

Award. In fact, he won two of them. In 2004, he won for his narration of *Peter and the Wolf.* The next year, he won for a reading of his own book *My Life.*

As a teenager in Hawaii, Barack Obama worked at a Baskin-Robbins ice cream parlor. He says he hasn't truly enjoyed ice cream since. He also collects Spider-Man and Conan the Barbarian comics.

Chapter 12

Everything That Happened after World War II

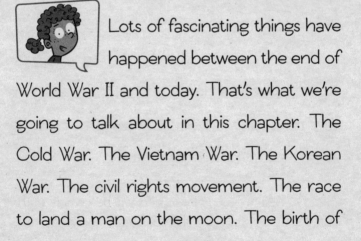

Lots of fascinating things have happened between the end of World War II and today. That's what we're going to talk about in this chapter. The Cold War. The Vietnam War. The Korean War. The civil rights movement. The race to land a man on the moon. The birth of rock and roll and hip-hop. The women's movement. The computer age. The internet. Terrorism. Cell phones . . . Bet you have a lot of weird fast facts about this recent history, right, Arlo?

 No! We can't talk about *any* of those things!

 Why not?

 We're running out of room in this book!* There are only a few more pages left! Now it's time to talk about important stuff. Like . . .

---

* But I have some good news. There will be a whole 'nother My Weird School Fast Facts book to cover all that stuff!

Chapter 13

The History of the Toilet!

Noooooooooooooo!

Yes, it's time! I've been waiting the whole book for this moment.

Do you *really* have to do this? I

find this subject to be disgusting.

Hey, I sat through all that boring stuff about who discovered America. Now you have to sit through *this*. Remember when Dr. Nicholas came to our class?* She told us that toilet bowls had been around for centuries. The first toilet you could *flush* was invented back in 1596 by a man named John Harrington. So he had the perfect name for a toilet bowl inventor: John.

Is this really important, Arlo?

_____

* Read *Dr. Nicholas Is Ridiculous!*

Yes! So anyway, in England in 1836 a baby was born, and his name was Tom Crapper. Yes, that was his real name! When Tom was fourteen, he went to work for a plumber in London. By the time he was twenty-five, he owned his own plumbing shop. Back in those days only very rich people owned a toilet. During the 1880s, Tom Crapper improved on the flushing toilet bowl. He

 also opened up a shop and sold toilet bowls to the public. For the first time, regular people could go to the store and buy a toilet bowl.

What a wonderful world! Hooray for Tom Crapper!

 That's such an inspirational story, Arlo. It brings tears to my eyes.

 I know lots of other stuff about toilets too.

 I bet you do.

During the Victorian era, people were constantly worried about their toilets exploding. They were afraid that flammable gasses in the liquid, caused by a build-up of waste in the sewage, would combine with a lit candle or cigarette that would ignite and blow up the toilet!

That's a crucial fast fact for kids to memorize. I hope the

readers are paying attention. You never know when this information might come in handy.

 Here's another one. The first president to have a toilet in the White House was John Quincy Adams in 1825. So John had a john!

 Charming. I'll remember that in case there's ever a test on this material.

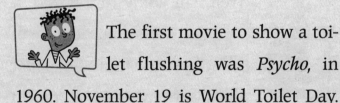 The first movie to show a toilet flushing was *Psycho*, in 1960. November 19 is World Toilet Day.

Most American toilets flush in the key of E flat.

 I can't believe you looked this stuff up.

 Do you know who invented toilet paper, Andrea?

 I really don't want to know, Arlo.

 Well, I'm going to tell you. It was a Massachusetts man named Joseph Gayetty. His toilet paper was introduced in 1857. It came in packages of flat sheets, and his name was printed on each sheet.

What did they use before 1857?

Believe me, Andrea, that's something you *really* don't want to know. But toilet paper on a *roll* was introduced by the Scott Paper Company in 1890. I don't think it was perfected back then though, because in 1935 a company called Northern Tissue invented "splinter-free" toilet paper. Ouch! More than seven *billion* rolls of toilet paper are sold every year in the United States. The average person uses more than twenty-three rolls a year!

 I'm not listening anymore, Arlo.

 Good. Don't. In Taiwan there's a restaurant chain called Modern Toilet! The walls are covered with showerheads! Toilet bowl plungers hang from the ceilings! The food is served on miniature toilet bowls and the drinks in little urinals! The seats are actual (non-working) toilets!

In South Korea there's a Restroom Cultural Park. It's a theme park where the theme is . . . toilets! The main exhibition hall is shaped like a giant toilet bowl! The theme park is located at the former home of the mayor Sim Jae-Duck. In 2007, he formed the World Toilet Association, and he was known as Mr. Toilet.

Restroom Cultural Park

Near San Antonio, Texas, is the Toilet Seat Art Museum. It's a museum filled with artwork painted on toilet seats! Isn't that cool?

 I'm covering my ears.

 Our custodian, Miss Lazar, has a museum devoted to toilet bowl plungers. Nobody knows who invented that thing. But toilet plungers are lifesavers. In California, on three different occasions, people performed CPR using toilet plungers.

Trumpet players also use the suction cup of a toilet bowl plunger to make the sound of their instrument more like a human voice. They take the stick out first. It would be weird if they didn't.

Will you look at the time? We really need to—

Are you embarrassed to say the word "bathroom"? Here are some other ways to say it: "lavatory," "latrine," "outhouse," "restroom," "water closet," "powder room," "can," "head," "john," "potty," "throne," "washroom," "loo," "comfort station," "little boys' room," "privy," "commode," "thunderbox"—

Is it almost over?

Almost. Forty thousand Americans a year are involved in toilet-related injuries. I know what you're thinking. How could anyone possibly get hurt from a toilet? Well, some people fall into them. Others slip on their wet bathroom floor and hit their head on the toilet. Ouch! Others stand on the seat to reach something and fall down. People have even been bitten by spiders hiding under outhouse toilet seats.

 Oh great. One more thing to worry about.

 During World War II, a German submarine was sunk after the toilet broke! Water came into the sub, it created chlorine gas when it touched a battery, and the sub had to come to the surface. Then the Allied forces destroyed it.

 Okay! Thank you, Arlo, for that disgusting look at toilet history.

 You're welcome!

The Ending

 Okay, now you know *all* there is to know about American history. You can go play video games, eat ice cream, and make armpit farts for the rest of your life. Yippee!

 As usual, Arlo is totally wrong. There's *so* much history that we couldn't fit in this book. If you can learn about the history of the toilet, you can learn about the history of *anything*. You could learn about the history of rubber bands. The history of pizza. The history of underwear!

 The history of underwear? That sounds interesting. Maybe we should have included a Chapter 14.

See what I mean? Poke around. With an adult's help, go online and search for stuff. History is *really* interesting. You can also go to your local library and look for other books on subjects that interest you.

 Ugh, Andrea said the B word! Yuck! Disgusting! I think I'm gonna throw up!

 Oh, stop being silly, Arlo. You *know* you like to learn new things. You just won't admit it. Learning is cool. And the best part is you get to impress grown-ups with how smart you are. Maybe one of the kids reading this book will grow up to be a genius. Maybe a college will be named in honor of one of them. Maybe one of them will become an astronaut and be the first human to set foot on Mars. Maybe someday our readers will know as much stuff as we do.

 But it won't be easy!